elin o'Hara slavick

Cameramouth

SurVision Books

First published in 2018 by
SurVision Books
Dublin, Ireland
www.survisionmagazine.com

Copyright © Elin O'Hara Slavick, 2018

Cover image © Elin O'Hara Slavick, 2018

Design © SurVision Books, 2018

ISBN: 978-1-9995903-4-5

This book is in copyright. No part of this publication may be reproduced, stored in a retrieval system or transmitted in any form or by any means without the prior permission in writing from the publisher.

Acknowledgements

Grateful acknowledgement is made to the editors of the following, in which a number of these poems originally appeared:
"Going Home in Your Dreams", "Greek Bus", "Dead Ex-Father-In-Law", and "Dreaming of David": *Papers of Surrealism;* "A Dada Love Song", "Dada Digesting", and "Dada Flag": *SurVision.*

CONTENTS

Going Home in Your Dreams   5
Time   6
The French Countryside   8
A Dada Love Song   10
What I Loved Most...   11
Dada Digesting   12
Dada Fireworks   13
Raw Dada   14
Dada Is Sick   15
Dada Drizzle   16
Dada Flag   18
Dada Zone   20
Vote Dada!   21
The Early Greek Philosophers Thought About Dada   22
Japanese Dada   23
Red Kitchen   24
Greek Bus   26
Six Gun City   27
Dead Ex-Father-in-Law   28
The Man of Eleven Doors   29
Cameramouth   30
Dreaming of David   32

If our eyes were cameras, there would never be enough film.

Going Home in Your Dreams

There are three people in a room
talking about flying and how
as a last resort you swim,
kick air and slap clouds.

Two people sit against a wall
drinking tea, waving.
You know them as you
take the wind to the top of the door,
fall to the knob.

You are the one to fly
like a horse off a cliff,
straddling the lukewarm green sea.
You believe your limbs to be wings.

You hold them against yourself
and still you float.
A mystery. You knock on a door
upon which is written,
"A teaching man and his precious wife."

You enter laughing so wide
the table falls in.

Time

Time wrecked no ship wretch crash.
Holy tick blasted tock.
There is never enough,
reverent and guilty,
wrist disease wrap addict,
wall altar.

Eternity finds no sex,
no hiding farmers,
no young clock watchers,
no buried artists.
What time does find is far worse.

Time kicks up from immortal dust
more time eternal,
sick days of fake hell,
laugh gust,
this one woman banging.

Time, you are far too elusive,
escaping even our God.
Masses end, prayers break
like brittle pews.
You line coffins and yards
with that big fat bottomless gut.

Time, I break my watch.
I break my wrist.
I crack my walls.

I bust my clock.
You can have the beginning.
There will be no end.

Time straight sharp hitch wedged,
grounded in these heels.
We resist the whole and end
in heart wince and no opera.

Oh time of Indian summer hiss night
like fruit hanging – puncture your ego.
Die deflated.

The French Countryside

Claudius killed all his rabbits
last year and ate them
one by one.
He lives next door to his old farm
that he sold to a man with no memory.
The man bought the house,
painted abstract pictures for two years,
climbed up into the grand attic
with an ornate gold frame, fell,
and cracked his head open on the old floor.

The man's son collects empty bird nests
from the stable's ceiling
for me to place on a table
next to a baby carriage filled
with white cloth and a photograph
of a dead baby girl,
solarized, held down
with little pebbles.

One nest was not as empty as he thought.
The small eggs
are opening
for soft orange future birds.
He tries to put the nest back,
but his ladder falls
and the nest comes undone,
yolk and glue spilling on the stones.
He sweeps it all away.

The bird mother swoops in and out
of our bad dust stirred up.
Tonight the moon turns the hills
into dark blue smoke.

A Dada Love Song

What you say is just about the thing you want to say
like rubies in your hair I kiss whatever.
Come back until it is light.
When I dream, I take long steps
because the vessel is aching and tilted.
Let's go back over it, okay?
Waiting for one more stone to rise.

Spit it out –
    the rain of tongue,
    the mist of teeth,
    the moon of voice.

(Strong sense of smell.)
Spit like wildfire spits the night.

First things first –
listen, listen until you hear more
and another tide falls –
or is it the dream again –
the one about dusk and the mirror,
mirror and dusk?
Which is which?

I am a leaf falling in the
wrong direction,
turning around up the down staircase.

What I Loved Most were the Tiny Little Dada Eyeballs that Swam in the Back of his Head

Cigarettes of doubt
burn slowly, sometimes ten.

Vomit burns brown and gold,
wise and old.

Mi alma, mi Corazon,
when will it end?

One, two, three, four, five,
we do not care to drive.

Like a keeper of tornadoes,
skate lizards walk fast and wear wigs.

Fair like flocks of flagrant follies
circle the mouth profusely.

The sound of the road map unfolding,
my finger is bleeding.

Stop rusting in your rubble,
great big mules in Sunday bonnets leap for meat below.

Dada Digesting

Stop this digesting.
Turn down the air conditioner.
No one is too young to sound like a sewer.
(Melted black rats.)

A blister in my mouth
From the hot potato canoe.

Free food.
Mushrooms.

The waitress lent me a strobe light.

Dada Fireworks

Let's get this whole thing over with.
Sour milk.
Rotten rhododendrons.
Lark Heart Attack.

It can't be good.

Holiday ocean.
Fire twigs.
Squeeze the muck.

Hovering siren curdles.
Hard bread breath.

Raw Dada

Not a trace was left.
Five minutes later
roots and fruits were abolished.

The savages would probably be celebrating
into violent canyons,
over crag and peak,
fence of triumphant human purpose.

Electrocuted animals,
gas bombs laughing,
pyramids straggle the plain.

Dada Is Sick

Pools forbid.
Fruit jewels tempt.

Zonal pandemonium pools.

Flux forsythia.
Euphemistic absinthe pools.

HELL

Cyanide including rib.
Discipline drinking.
Spoiled stinking.
Zounds demanding serpents.

Dada Drizzle

We smoke more than we eat wheat.
Wrinkled and stained,
brown paper bags fall.

I will not lay beside you.

Earth quakes.
Oil melting across the lake.
Fools sawed in half.
The whole west coast shakes, swirls.

Oh Mother, I can feel the soil falling.

Icebergs of tar,
our president is heavy.
Two monsters:
Love and death.

Please do not swim to Valhalla.

Ladders of Nirvana sleep.
Bull under ships and forts.
Black Spanish hats, bottle caps,
hunchback town.
Trolls of Cairo.

Noise smells like trees drop.

The fast smell of ground ginger
uproots fish like lawn sprinklers.
The lady is dignified
under fluorescent weather.
She burns cut crops and
those stubborn pray like chaos.

Swimming over my head.

Society remembers a Sunday in 1973.
Sickle planting
steeple crosses
in the river.

Dada Flag

Fallen plants. Electric pigeons.
Worms – we waded backwards.

Swing bed
Croon face.

Whisper wasted shaking in the mud.
Survive like bones of infinity.
Piss off.
Suffer like Christ man.

Hell shoots.

O no state finding
injured flowers.

(Leather and radishes.)
Six feet under
but thousands of feet up.

Man like an apple core,
dead on the hill,
rotting Nicaraguan disembodied.

Political darkness
wading in the hatred.

Greek mortal boots,
devils grab your ankles.
(Sway themselves.)

Kings of the road-blocked road.
Others howl like LOVE.

So dangerous president,
vote for dirt –
you will always be standing upon earth,
molten.

Breakdown.
Assassination.

O Folk.
Women wave breast like flags
of patriotic puppets.
The government is wading.

My God's gonna take care of all sides.

Dada Zone

One of those bombs that blows up people,
but not buildings.

Knitting clay head.
Smooth daze.
Lazy lawn trippers,
stumbling throat,
drop it now.

Fringe cough pulp.
Sparks drooling fast.
Drop it psychic heaven.
Swirl bleached stones.

Vote Dada!

The streets are paved with rain
in the south no more.
Exhausting damn Reagan,
sick man,
that big fat bank bulge below this country's belt,
his rusted pitchfork like an old belly.
Southern rain has gone dry
like a red river bed,
hard gutter gulley.
The popular crown themselves.

Crown no one.

Sonic booms, olives, termites and hedgehogs.
The money is buried in the forest.
The Delta Queen rolls like butter down the Mississippi,
Russians waving at Americans waving from the bank,
crawling on their bellies,
thinking of hanging upside down.

Saying good-bye is impossible
unless you become an octopus,
cranking mad ocean gone under.
The water will go your way politically.
Shatterhouse, frozen iron, half-life, damn old government.

94% censored.
6% fist.

The Early Greek Philosophers Thought About Dada

Twisted tables, incidental chairs.
What wishes were insane, asylum?
The train, the sane lover
craning her neck again,
again my friend is a moron.

I bled a puddle –
then I knew I cared.
My glasses were bubbles.
My tears could not escape.
Building, block of mules bursting;
bored with bubbles.
Years from now,
I'll think of you, your shining hair,
and crazy frock and angels.

Oh rainbow gills, don't fly
so fast! Like mimes being raped,
egg bread.
Babble tower roast,
dark dinner of my lover.
Screaming harlequins.
This can get very scary.

Japanese Dada

Monsoon cucumbers need graves.
Please sweat.

Rufus drinks whiskey.
Marshes soaking,
black cloud over the bank.
Tweed.

Electric jug coffin dilemma.

Flamingo miso.
We like mosquitoes dropping.
Bank dates.

Film bamboo fast.
Sushi because spoons,
thunder patriots.

Twisted bamboo.

Bamboo in bamboo.
Bamboo Siddhartha.

Red Kitchen

I want them both.
Crackface.
Perpetual, perpetual, perpetual.
Stabbing movie stills
and pills like foreign horses.

Mercy me.
Tongue of confusion.
Lust, curb that lust.
Wisdom smells funny.
Split heart, we breed.

His horns are beautiful.
Broken knuckled trees
of women like bandits,
darkrooms, crashed breasts of the girls I love.
Black couch,
stewed breath
in a once again hectic life.

The horseman falls
because of the feasting ladies
dropping dead gorgeous.

Lung dust,
a sound is not an ocean.
We meet as big feelings.
The lack of a different state,
tomato, barley and tarragon
for the death of a dinosaur.
Blood, curb that in a vein.

Greek Bus

Flowers suck ivory dry to dust.
Exhaust chokes the ocean
and the lady with her legs up on the seat,
collecting sun in the lap of her dress,
sews her fingers into the hem
while her husband counts the hairs on his legs.

Nothing is happening.
The ocean licks itself clean
like the night cat sucking rabbit bones dry.
Distance never measures itself.

Six Gun City

Men pick nuts from the shells
with the crack of their teeth,
an empty glass of warm vodka
on the kitchen counter,
cat in heat.

His car is low.
One woman hides her chest
while she drives,
putting on her seatbelt
and taking it off
just in time to go through the light.

She does not know where she is going
or how long it has been since the rain.
He is driving in circles,
his gun shifting across maps
in the glove compartment like an old bone.

Dead Ex-Father-in-Law

The day breeds us late,
old heavy animals dragging
from one small room to tiny other.
We collect gold leaf
and blank paper,
our skin stained with dust.

We do not know
what to do with our time
so we sift through
a dead man's photographs –
half naked women
pretending to be dead,
tied to the tracks in high heels,
buried on the stone beach up to the ankles
or hanging upside down,
bones shifting under gravity,
unable to tell the difference
between blood and blush,
gravity and artificial wind.

The photographs of his family
are evidence of the time
before the blindness.
We carry boxes of pornography
and linen to the street.

The Man of Eleven Doors

For José Esteban Muñoz, 1988

The first door is smoke
and the second is confetti
like broken seeds
falling from his lips.

The door behind him is third and wrong,
unlike the fourth of Formica from Florida,
smooth with obligation to the past.

He has five feet and six shoes
in his closet of books
like finger holes in his socks,
like dust on the needle.

His seventh holiday is locked
in the eighth moon –
a tilted committee.

The next doors are one,
a solitary hatchet counting
one, one, one.

The eleventh door is his soul,
teeth and all,
pulling the pulp of fruit.

Cameramouth

There was never a photograph
of an old camera with bellows
with teeth at the top and bottom
of the lens,
French scrawled across the back
in blue cursive ink.

I never lost the photograph
at the counter of the antique store
when I went to pay for it.
No one waiting
in line behind me stole it.

It was just gone.
And it was never there.

Hovering between sleep and dreams,
a gift I wanted to buy for a student
who photographs everything:
rotten fruit, airplane wings,
deer statues and old greyhounds.

I wake to empty hands
digging in the dirt
for the treasure
of emulsion and collage,
the uncanny object,
a hungry and oral camera
that eats

speaks
devours
tastes
screams
licks
and bites auras –
those illuminated traces
of what once was there, here,
nowhere and everywhere.

Dreaming of David

A poet standing on a platform
in front of a crowd of miners
at a funeral service for a workers poet said,
"We are not today
what we were yesterday."

The workers shouted, "Speak clearly.
We do not understand you."
The poet said, "Today is not like yesterday.
We have lost our red violin."
Everyone knew the red violin
was the dead poet
who wrote poems
they would play
on their violins.

The workers shouted,
"Speak clearly. We cannot understand you."
The poet tried again,
"We can't hear the red violin."
The miners shouted back,
"The blue today is as blue as blue.
The sand beneath our feet
when we come up from underground
is the sound of a thousand
triangles being murdered."

The poet stopped.
He knew this was the dead poet's poem.
The poet picked up the violin and started playing.

www.ingramcontent.com/pod-product-compliance
Lightning Source LLC
Chambersburg PA
CBHW061315040426
42444CB00010B/2647